A GIFT FOR

_____

FROM

_____

Who is this Jesus?

A portion of this book first appeared in
Tell Me the Story written by Max Lucado
and published by Crossway Books.

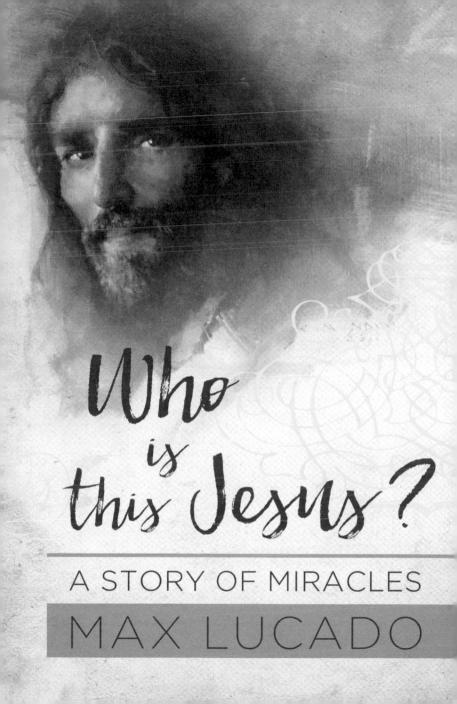

Who is this Jesus?

A STORY OF MIRACLES

MAX LUCADO

Published by Worthy Inspired, an imprint of Worthy Publishing Group, a division of Worthy Media, Inc., One Franklin Park, 6100 Tower Circle, Suite 210, Franklin, TN 37067.

HELPING PEOPLE EXPERIENCE THE HEART OF GOD
eBook available at worthypublishing.com

Library of Congress Control Number: 2013932683

Unless otherwise noted, Scripture quotations are taken from the Holy Bible, *New International Version*. Copyright © 1973, 1978, 1984 by Biblica, Inc.™ Used by permission of Zondervan. All rights reserved worldwide.

Scripture quotations marked MSG are taken from *The Message*. Copyright © 1993, 1994, 1995, 1996, 2000, 2001, 2002. Used by permission of NavPress Publishing Group.

Scripture quotations marked NRSV are taken from the *New Revised Standard Version Bible*. Copyright © 1989 the Division of Christian Education of the National Council of the Churches of Christ in the United States of America. Used by permission. All rights reserved.

Publisher's Acknowledgment

The publisher wishes to acknowledge that a portion of the text for this book originally appeared in *Tell Me the Story* written by Max Lucado and published by Crossway Books. This updated and expanded edition features original artwork by C. Michael Dudash.

For foreign and subsidiary rights, contact Riggins International Rights Services, Inc.; rigginsrights.com

ISBN: 978-1-61795-853-3 (hardcover)

Cover Design: Melissa Reagan
Interior Layout : Bart Dawson
Cover and Interior Art: C. Michael Dudash

Printed in China

16 17 18 19 20 21 HAHA 8 7 6 5 4 3 2 1

FOR MARIE SHIPP

AND MARIA DUTTON

May the promise of resurrection

morning gild your days.

There is hope
in your difficult
situation.

EDITOR'S INTRODUCTION

Just for a moment,
picture the worst day of your life.

Do you remember any of the details?

Where you were, who was with you,
what was said, how you felt?

The planet earth had a worst day too. But here's the interesting thing: That day didn't take God by surprise. He already knew what he intended to do. In fact, it was his plan all along to take that Worst Day of All and make it the Best Day of All. How did he do it? Well, doing impossible things has always been a part of God's resume.

In this little book, author Max Lucado will take a closer look at the-worst-day-that-became-the-best-day and, Max being Max, he will do so from an unexpected angle.

The fact is, when Jesus died and then came out of the grave three days later, it put every bad day you will ever have in a completely different light. If the blackest and most terrible day ever led directly to the most joyous and hope-filled day that could ever be . . . well, then, maybe there is hope for the difficult situations you find yourself facing.

One of the most encouraging things about the Bible is that it assumes we will have setbacks, heartaches, failures, mountain-sized disappointments, and great difficulties in the course of our lives. Then it meets us right where we are (wherever that might be) with the exact hope and help we've been longing for but didn't think we could ever find.

Hope: in the best of times,
  and the worst of times.

Now imagine a lonely fugitive with a death sentence on his head, wrongly accused of crimes he never committed, forced to hide from the authorities in the impenetrable darkness of a limestone cave. But then, you don't have to imagine it, because it really happened.

That was the story of David, a young army officer who aroused the king's jealousy and found himself running for his life for over fifteen years.

The book of Psalms records his heart's cry, where he writes:

> "When my spirit grows faint within me, it is you who know my way. . . . No one is concerned for me. I have no refuge; no one cares for my life. I cry to you, O Lord; I say, 'You are my refuge.'" (142:3–5)

When David came to the very end of himself—the ragged, frayed, played-out end of his hopes, on his face, in a dark cave—he fell into an understanding that would keep him strong for the rest of his life:

God was his refuge,

　　　　his hiding place, and his hope,

no matter what happened to him

　　　　　　in life or in death.

Many centuries later, a distressed, beat-up missionary named Paul arrived at the same conclusion—with the same result. Listen to the words that he penned (with a shaking hand?) in a letter to friends:

"We don't want you in the dark, friends, about how hard it was when all this came down on us.... It was so bad we didn't think we were going to make it. We felt like we'd been sent to death row, that it was all over for us. As it turned out, it was the best thing that could have happened. Instead of trusting in our own strength or wits to get out of it, we were forced to trust God totally—not a bad idea since he's the God who raises the dead! And he did it, rescued us from certain doom. And he'll do it again, rescuing us as many times as we need rescuing" (2 Corinthians 1:8–11 MSG).

That's a really big idea in the Bible, from one cover to the other.

God opens unseen doors in what we thought were dead-ends. God yanks open curtains in dark rooms where we didn't even know there was a window. God takes terrible, intolerable, impossible situations and finds a way to walk his kids through the worst of them, leading them to surprising vistas and unexpected destinations.

The Bible has examples of this on almost every page, but one tops them all. In fact, one story makes all those other stories of hope possible.

Don't call it "Easter," unless you want to make every day "Easter." This is about the one miracle that has opened the door for all miracles.

J ohn launches his Gospel account before day-light, just as the first hint of gray has crept onto the eastern horizon.

The first character he mentions is the mysterious Mary Magdalene who finds her way through the darkness to the tomb of Jesus. Was she carrying a little oil lamp that cast shadows on the path? Were her eyes blurred with tears? Was she afraid of encountering those stern Roman soldiers who stood guard over that grave, or was her heart so torn by grief that she no longer cared what happened to her?

There came a moment when she turned a corner and saw in that dim, gray light what her eyes at first refused to believe. Did her hand tremble as she held up her little oil lamp?

The soldiers were gone and the tomb was wide open. A cavernous hole yawned before her, midnight-black in those dark moments before dawn.

There was no joy in this.

Not yet.

This was vandalism.

A sacrilege.

An unthinkable, unspeakable desecration.

Grave robbery.

Someone had taken the body of her dead Lord. Someone had actually broken into his tomb and carried away his remains. For what purpose? To make a mockery of him? To heap further indignities on the corpse of this best-of-all men who had been so kind and good and true?

Dropping the lamp, she began to run. And run and run and run. She had to find Peter. Or John. Or both. They would know what to do. Did she pound on some door to awaken the men . . . or had the disciples been keeping watch, perhaps sitting by the low coals of a fire that had burned all night long? Again, the Bible doesn't say, but . . . can we imagine some outrage in Mary Magdalene's voice?

"They have taken the Lord out of the tomb, and we don't know where they have put him!"

John 20:2

It was a Sunday morning that had been, that would be, filled to the brim with drama, wonder, angels, consternation, weeping—and incredulous, almost uncontainable joy.

But there was also controversy.

The news that overwhelmed the followers of Jesus with such overwhelming awe was the worst news possible for the Jewish leaders who thought they had dealt with the Nazarene and put him behind them once and for all.

And what of the Roman soldiers who had been blasted off their feet by a powerful earthquake and the appearance of a mighty angel—bright as a lightning flash—who pushed back the stone that had covered the tomb?

The Bible doesn't tell the story of any of these soldiers—what they thought, how they recovered from the shock of their lives, and what they might have wondered in the hours and days that followed. It is one of those stories we may have to wait until heaven to ask about.

And yet . . .

If the story could have been told . . .

If the story had been told . . .

It might have gone something like this . . .

Who is this Jesus?

MAX LUCADO

T ell it, you say? Tell it again?
I've told you all I know.
I've even told what I don't know."

"But some are just arriving. They haven't heard what you saw. Tell us again."

The heavy door opened and shut quickly as two more men entered the small room. Claudius supposed this was a storage room, but he wasn't sure. It was too dark.

The only light was a slit of afternoon sunshine creeping through an opening in the wooden shutters and streaking across the faces of the listeners.

The group numbered fifteen, maybe twenty—about as many men as women. A few men were shaven, most bearded. A few asked questions. A few shook their heads.

All sat with eyes fixed on the young soldier
whose story they longed to hear but didn't
know whether to believe.

Claudius took a breath and began his story again. "I wasn't supposed to work that night. I'd worked over the Sabbath and was tired. In fact, I had been on duty since Friday morning."

"I remember your face." The voice belonged to a woman sitting on the floor. "You were on the hill."

"I was assigned to Golgotha detail a month ago."

A grumble went up from the group.

Claudius defended himself.

"I didn't ask for it. I was given it."

Emotion was thick in the room, but then someone was urging,

"Go on, finish the story!"

Claudius again shifted his weight. He would never have imaged himself in a room full of Jews.

The contrast between his trimmed hair and short uniform and their beards and robes only added to his discomfort. He eyed his spear on the floor at his feet. His Roman shield leaned against the adobe wall.

*Coming here
was a dangerous move.*

He had been uneasy ever since he arrived in Jerusalem a few months back. Certainly wasn't his choice of a place to serve, but when Rome sends, a soldier obeys.

Besides, he told himself, a year in a peaceful outpost couldn't be too bad.

Wrong, Jerusalem was far from peaceful.

The Jews hated the soldiers. The soldiers distrusted the Jews. If it wasn't the priests' complaints, it was the zealots' riots. Forget casual strolls down the street keeping peace. Jerusalem was a hotbed of anger.

Anger at Rome.

Anger at the world.

They called themselves the people of God.
Some nation of God!

No navy.

Puny army.

No emperor.

Just a temple, a Torah, and some strange
rules about the Sabbath.

Claudius had been trained to respect strength
and size—neither of which he found here.

Until last night.

What he saw last night he'd never seen in Rome or anywhere else. When he told his officers about it, they told him to keep quiet. He couldn't. He had to have some answers. So he came here. These people wanted answers, too. So they let him in.

They were easy to find. Every soldier in the city knew where they were hiding—the upper room of the large white corner house. It was the same place they had met last week when he was still here.

One by one they had drifted back to the room—each entering with a knock on the door and a shameful nod. When Claudius learned how they had run away and left Jesus alone, he was amazed that they had returned. "Why are you still here then?" he had asked. "Why don't you go home?"

"If you'd seen him do what we've seen him do, you would stay, too," a disciple explained.

"Sounds like he has," added another.

For by now they all knew what had happened at the tomb. Or better, they knew something had happened at the tomb. No one quite knew how to explain it. Claudius picked up his story where he'd left off.

"When I first saw him being led up the hill, I noticed he was different. He didn't demand we let him go. He didn't shout or resist. And when we hammered the spike into his hand—"

Claudius paused, wondering if he should have mentioned this.

An encouraging nod from one of the women told him to continue. "When we placed the spike in his hand, he held his hand still. He didn't fight."

"Sounds like something he would do," a man in the back stated. Several nodded in agreement.

"He never seemed angry." Claudius' voice grew softer as he continued. "He never blamed anyone. People were cursing and laughing at him, but not once did I see his eyes lose their calm."

No one moved as Claudius spoke. When he had shared these events with his superiors earlier in the day, they had scoffed. It didn't matter to the Romans how Jesus had acted. But it mattered to these people. They wanted to know every detail.

For the first time, Claudius felt a camaraderie with his listeners—a camaraderie based on a fascination with one man.

He continued, "'Forgive them,' I heard him say. And when he spoke, I looked up. He was looking at me. His face was a mask of blood and spit. But he was praying for me."

The only movement in the room was the nodding of heads.

"After the crucifixion I helped lower the body and lay it on the ground. I waited as these women—" He motioned to several near the front. "I waited as they prepared the body, and then I saw that it was placed in the tomb."

"I thought my day was over. I took four men
to close the grave's opening with a huge stone.
When we turned to leave, word came that
Pilate and the temple leaders were nervous that
someone would steal the body. We were told to
seal the tomb and stand guard all night."

"There were several of us; so we built a fire and took turns. I was the first to sleep. When they woke me for my turn, it was an hour before dawn.

"The night was black—as black as any night I can remember. The moon was small, and the stars were hidden by the clouds.

"I stood on one side. Another soldier stood on the other. He laughed about how easy it was to guard a tomb. Not often does a soldier get guard duty in a cemetery. Maybe we dozed off, but at first I thought I was dreaming. The ground began to shake—violently. It shook so hard I fell to the ground."

"Rocks fell from the walls behind us.

Sparks flew from the fire.

The soldiers asleep on the ground jumped up.
I know they were standing because when the
light hit them, I could see their faces like it was
broad daylight."

"What light?" someone asked.

"You tell me!" Claudius demanded.

"Where did that light come from? The rock rolled back, and the light roared out. A burst of fire with no heat. A gust of wind blew from the tomb, put out the fire, knocked us back, and the next thing I knew,

the tomb was empty.

I looked at the soldiers.

They were stunned.

About that time these two women appeared."

"That's when we saw the angel!"

Mary blurted.

"He was sitting on the rock!
He told us that Jesus was not there.
He told us that..."

She hesitated, knowing her words would be hard to believe.

"He told us that Jesus is no longer dead!"

Her words rang in the room like a peal of a bell. No one dared to speak. Finally one did.

A clean-shaven younger man said softly, but firmly,

"Just like he said he would."

"You mean,

he said he would do this?"

Claudius asked.

"More than once. But we didn't understand.
We didn't believe. Until today."

"John," one of the women asked the man
speaking, "you were there. You went to the
tomb. Is that what you say?"

"Peter and I saw the tomb. We saw it open
and empty.

But we didn't see Jesus."

Once again the room was quiet. Then Claudius broke the silence.

"I have a question.

"I've told you what you wanted to know. Now you tell me what I want to know. This has been on my mind all weekend. It's been on my heart ever since I struck the nail into Jesus' hand.

"Who is this man?

Who is this Jesus?"

If any head had hung before, it lifted at this moment. If any thoughts had wandered, they wandered no more.

"Is there any doubt?" Mary said. Her eyes were bright. She jumped to her feet as she spoke.

"I saw him! I saw him risen from the dead. He is who he said he is. He is the Son of God!"

With that statement the room broke into chaos.

"Impossible!"

"No, she's right. Let her speak!"

"Why did he let them kill him
if he is the Son of God?"

"It doesn't make sense."

*"What doesn't make sense
is why you can't believe!"*

Claudius was silent. What he was hearing, he could not handle. But what he had seen at the grave, he could not deny. He leaned over and put his elbows on his knees and buried his face in his hands.

Thoughts rumbled in his head. He was so intent that he didn't notice the sudden silence. Stillness reigned for several seconds before he raised his head.

A light filled the room.

> *He looked at the door and the window; they were still closed.*

Faces that had been cast in shadows now beamed. All eyes stared in his direction— not at him but behind him. But before he could turn to see what they were seeing, a hand was on his shoulder. When Claudius turned to look at the hand, he found the answer for his heart.

The hand was pierced.

EDITOR'S EPILOGUE

Stillness reigned for several seconds...

A light filled the room. He looked at the door and the window; they were still closed.

It was late on a Sunday night, and fear seeped into the room like a cold mist. The small group of Christ-followers inside had barred the doors. It was whispered and rumored that the authorities had determined to stamp out every last vestige of the Nazarene sect, even if it meant stonings or more executions. Their informants, of course, were everywhere.

The disciples spoke in low tones, barely above a whisper, and took care to avoid the windows. What they needed was a plan—some sort of rudimentary course to follow in the coming days.

No one, however, made the attempt. How could you plan when your world had been splintered into a thousand pieces?

And then, without a sound, there he was, standing in their midst.

"Peace be with you!"

he said, and he didn't whisper.

This was something new. And just a little bit startling. The resurrected Jesus Christ would now step into closed rooms without the benefit of a door or window. The Gospel of John records two instances, one week apart. In the book of Luke, the two disciples who had encountered Jesus on the road to Emmaus were just getting ready to tell their story to the others when the Lord himself showed up, with the same greeting, "Peace be with you" (Luke 24:36 NRSV).

Years later, when the apostle Paul sat alone, head in hands, in a guardroom inside the Roman army barracks in Jerusalem, he suddenly looked up to see that he had a visitor.

The Bible says: "That night the master appeared to Paul: 'It's going to be all right. Everything is going to turn out for the best. You've been a good witness for me here in Jerusalem. Now you're going to be my witness in Rome!'" (Acts 23:11 MSG).

It really doesn't matter if it's a locked room or a holding cell under guard; Jesus will still come to be near his brothers and sisters. He will stand close to them and say, "Don't be afraid. It's going to be all right. Everything is going to turn out for the best."

It might be in a hospital room at night, in the midst of wires, tubes, and monitors. It might be in a dark prison in some forsaken corner of the world. It might be on some lonely night in a small apartment, with rain beating against the windows. It might even be on the moon, as astronaut James Irwin experienced God's tangible presence some 240,000 miles from home.

Jesus still enters locked rooms, tight places, and desolate corners of our world. He will go anywhere to be with his loved ones. It doesn't matter if it's in a nursing home or an ICU. It makes no difference if it's in a palace, a guest room at the White House, the back booth of some greasy spoon cafe late in the wee hours, or a dusty, nondescript motel room on the back side of nowhere.

The "where" just doesn't matter to him.

It's the "who" that matters, and you are that who.

In the book of Hebrews he declares,
          "Never will I leave you;
            never will I forsake you" (13:15).
And to all his followers everywhere he promises,
          "Surely I am with you always,
            to the very end of the age" (Matthew 28:20).

This is the hope we have—

always in our best of times, and especially in our
worst of times.

Nothing can keep Jesus from those he loves.
          Not life and not death.
          Nothing in heaven, earth, or hell.

He proved that on resurrection day, and he
will go on proving it forever.

"And we rejoice in the hope of the glory of God.
Not only so, but we also rejoice in our sufferings,
because we know that suffering
produces perseverance;
perseverance, character;
and character, hope.
And hope does not disappoint us,
because God has poured out
his love into our hearts. . . ."

ROMANS 5:2–4

MAX LUCADO is a *New York Times* and *USA Today* best-selling author of nearly 100 books with 80 million copies in print. A three-time recipient of the Christian Book of the Year Award, Lucado was named "America's Pastor" by *Christianity Today* and "The Best Preacher in America" by *Reader's Digest.* He is a minister of preaching at Oak Hills Church in San Antonio, where he has served since 1988. He and his wife, Denalyn, have been married over thirty years and have three grown daughters and one son-in-law.

C. MICHAEL DUDASH has been a full-time oil painter and illustrator since 1977. His work in the publishing arena has been used by hundreds of clients over the years and has won him numerous awards and a widespread reputation as a master painter. Much of his work has been centered on Christian subject matter and the creation of contemporary artwork that illustrates the Gospel. Dudash lives with his wife, Valerie, in the Coeur d'Alene, Idaho, area, where he works out of his home and studio. To see more of his artwork, go to cmdudash.com.

IF YOU ENJOYED THIS BOOK, WILL YOU CONSIDER SHARING THE MESSAGE WITH OTHERS?

Mention the book in a blog post or through Facebook, Twitter, Pinterest, or upload a picture through Instagram.

Recommend this book to those in your small group, book club, workplace, and classes.

Head over to facebook.com/worthypublishing, "LIKE" the page, and post a comment as to what you enjoyed the most.

Tweet "I recommend reading #WhoIsThisJesus by @MaxLucado // @worthypub"

Pick up a copy for someone you know who would be challenged and encouraged by this message.

Write a book review online.

WORTHY®
PUBLISHING

Visit us at worthypublishing.com

twitter.com/worthypub

worthypub.tumblr.com

facebook.com/worthypublishing

pinterest.com/worthypub

instagram.com/worthypub

youtube.com/worthypublishing